Environmental Lifestyle Guide

For Grade 9 Students

VOL.1 OF 11

FOOD

Jahangir Asadi

Vancouver, BC CANADA

Copyright © 2022 by **SILOSA** Consulting Group Inc.

Published by: Silosa Consulting Group Inc.
Vancouver, BC **CANADA**
Email: Info@Silosa.ca
www.silosa.ca

Ordering Information:
Quantity sales. Special discounts are available on quantity purchases by universities, schools, corporations, associations, and others. For details, contact the "Sales Department" at the above mentioned email address.

Environmental lifestyle Guide Vol.1 for Grade.9/J.Asadi —1st ed.
ISBN: 978-1-990451-75-1

Contents

We hope that, 10,000 years from now, future generations
will be able to see flowers that provide bees with nectar
and pollen and...
BEES provide flowers with the means to reproduce by
spreading pollen from flower to flower,....

Jahangir Asadi

This book is dedicated to my professor, Dr.Sadeq Fakhr

The more you care about our environment, the more it will be protected from contaminants and toxins

Introduction

This book is part of an eleven volume series that is meant to be a standard text-book series, for grades 9 to 12. TTAIN & ESFK & SCG improves quality of life and reduces environmental degradation by fostering new consumption patterns and sustainable lifestyles through International Cooperative Extension Service programs at houses, offices, schools and libraries all over the globe.

Climate change is real. Therefore people have the potential to make a difference now and for future generations. This book provides climate science basics, including the roles that lifestyles and populations play in the climate scenario, the significance of carbon footprints, and an overview of the current climate situation. The manual has been categorized based on humanity's needs starting first with food and ending with tourism. The manual then illustrates the difference between adaptation (taking steps to live with the changes) and mitigation (taking steps to slow the rate of change.)

Adaptation examples include food, energy, transportation, recreation. Mitigation focuses on effectively engaging with local governments, through serving on advisory boards, communicating with public officials, educational institutes, schools, universities, libraries and leading communities towards climate change actions.

One useful way to mitigate climate change is through increasing public knowledge to better understand the impact of the rate of change on plants and animals. This is crucial for preserving species; and for assessing potential insects and disease outbreaks in agriculture, natural resources and public health.

Taking personal action is a key element of this manual.

Citizens are challenged to consume 20% fewer resources, to bring world consumption levels down as much as possible. Readers are given 12 practical steps to take to make the changes. The resources section provides additional information, and readers are encouraged to contact the author for further questions.

As an accessibility action, we have provided Online international courses on climate change control as well. You can access the courses via the following link:

http://TopTenAward.org

SILOSA Consulting Group (SCG)

Silosa Consulting Group (SCG) was established to provide outstanding consulting services of management system & educational standards to individuals, groups, companies, schools, and organizations all over the globe. SCG is publishing an "Environmental Lifestyle Guide " book series as a standard textbook related to increasing environmental awareness of students means being aware of the natural environment and making choices that benefit the earth, rather than hurt it. Vol.1 to 11 (for grades 9 to 12) providing some of the ways to practice environmental awareness include: **Recycling**, **Conserving energy and water**, **Reuse, Activism, and others**.

SCG book publishing services and distribution services are connected to over 39,000 booksellers worldwide, including Apple, Amazon, Barnes & Noble, Indigo, Google Play Books, and many more. SCG has enough experiences to help create new and effective environmental educational programmes in different countries all over the world. For more detail, visit our website : http://silosa.ca and/or send your enquirer to the following email:

info@silosa.ca

CHAPTER 1

About ISO 14000 for Students

The International Organization for Standardization is an independent, non-governmental organization, the members of which are the standards organizations of the 165 member countries. It is the world's largest developer of voluntary international standards and it facilitates world trade by providing common standards among nations. More than twenty thousand standards have been set, covering everything from manufactured products and technology to food safety, agriculture, and healthcare.

Kids ISO 14000s
"Kids ISO 14000s" is a new environmental education program for children, based on ISO 14000s, which is international standard for environmental management. Primary aims of this program are: -
1. To teach and train children how to manage the environmental issues (such as energy saving) by themselves through the working book and guide book of this program,
2. To certify those children who showed good accomplishment in the program from highly international authority (as is the case of ISO 14000s)
3. To network those children through the international network (Kids International Network), so that the children can work on the environment, internationally.

2. System of Kids ISO 14000s Program
The system of Kids ISO 14000s Program consists of
1. Operation Headquarter (ArTech).
2. Workbook, Guidebook (originally published by ArTech, and local versions are produced by each countries).
3. Eco-Kids-Instructors for local operation and evaluation of the performance of the children.
4. International accreditation committee for accreditation of accomplishment of the children, for certification of the Eco-Kids-Instructors, as well as overall checks of this program.
5. Linkage with international organizations (such as UNU, UNESCO, etc. ...) And also national organizations

More information can be obtained :

www.ISO.org

Canada

Environmental Sustain for Future kids established in Vancouver, BC Canada in 2020. (ESFK) is an international ecolabel focused on taking care of environment for future of kids. ESFK defined as 'self-declared' environmental claims made by manufacturers and businesses based on ISO 14020 series of standards, the claimant can declare the environmental objectives and targets in relation to taking care of environment for future kids. However, this declaration will be verifiable.

Environmental Sustain for Future Kids
Vancouver, BC CANADA

Email: info@esfk.org
Web: www.esfk.org

STEP ONE

Food & Recycling

As an average person drinks 60,000 liters in a lifetime, we are recycling water ourselves. While polluting our oceans we are poisoning our children and grandchildren. Water is natures most vital resource. Let's work together to prevent further pollution of our oceans. Currently, just 25% of mobile phones can be recycled right now. A total of 3.4 million tonnes of plastics were consumed in Australia. A total of 320 000 tonnes of plastics were

recycled, which is an increase of 10 per cent from the 2016-17 recovery. Recycling just one ton of aluminum cans conserves more than 152 million Btu, the equivalent of 1,024 gallons of gasoline or 21 barrels of oil consumed. The universal recycling symbol, logo or icon is an internationally recognized symbol used to designate recyclable materials. The recycling symbol is in the public domain and is not a trademark.

Step Up: Recycle, Reuse & Reduce
How can I recycle?

STEP 1: Go Green & Recycle
Separate recyclables from your trash with a recycling bin. Such as a dual trash can with two compartments or a compost bin. But you can also use a paper shredder for sorting sensitive paperwork that needs shredding before you recycle it. By using these recycling tools you prevent the loss of recyclable materials.

STEP 2: Go Green & Reuse
Plastic disposables and single-use products are wasteful and not stylish. Be fashionable and more eco-friendly and bring your own beautiful and reusable essentials such as a reusable water bottle, coffee cup or fold-able shopping bag. Make a trendy statement and stop plastic pollution.

STEP 3: Go Green & Reduce
How do you reduce plastics and prevent plastic pollution? The answer is: use more natural resources. This is also known as living a zero waste lifestyle where the mission is to reduce waste as much as possible. Check our zero waste store with eco-friendly paper straws, bamboo toothbrushes, and metal safety razors.

STEP 4: Team Up & Go Green
Start a Green Team in your office or workplace together with your colleagues to educate, inspire, challenge and empower employees about your sustainability goals. Know what you throw away today in the office and think about how you and your colleagues can reduce, reuse and recycle tomorrow.

Why is a green lifestyle important?

Nature can't digest plastics because this material is not biodegradable. We can use much more natural resources that are biodegradable by nature itself. Because not 100% of what we consume will be collected or recycled.

The three arrows of the recycling symbol represent the three main stages of the recycling process: recycling, reusing and reducing. These three chasing arrows are also known as the recycling trilogy, and Together the arrows form a closed loop that symbolizes a circular economy.

What is recycling?

Recycling is the process of collecting and processing materials that would otherwise be thrown away as trash and turning them into new products. Recycling can benefit your community, the economy and the environment.

Is recycling truly beneficial for the environment?

The answer is Yes, For example:

Recycling 500 kg of paper can save the energy equivalent of consuming 160 gallons of gasoline.

Recycling just 1000 kg of aluminum cans conserves 1,000 gallons of gasoline or more than 20 barrels of oil consumed.

Plastic bottles are the most recycled plastic product in the United States as of 2015, according to our most recent report. Recycling just 10 plastic bottles saves enough energy to power a laptop for more than 25 hours.

Why is it important to only put items that can be recycled in the recycling bin?

Putting items in the recycling bin that can't be recycled can contaminate the recycling stream. After these unrecyclable items arrive at recycling centers, they can cause costly damage to the equipment. Additionally, after arriving at recycling centers, they must be sorted out and then sent to landfills, which raises costs for the facility. That is why it is important to check with your local recycling provider to ensure that they will accept certain items before placing them into a bin. Some items may also be accepted at retail locations or other at local recycling centers.

Why are some items that look recyclable not accepted at my recycling facility?

Your local recycling facility might not accept all recyclable items. This is especially true with plastics. While plastic bottles are the most commonly recycled plastic products, other plastics may or may not be accepted in your area, so first check what your local recycling provider accepts. It is important to understand that the existence of a plastic resin code on the product does not guarantee that the product is recyclable in your area. Additionally, glass may not be accepted in some areas, so please confirm with your local provider.

What should I never put in my recycling bin(s)?

Garden hoses
Sewing needles
Bowling balls
Food or food-soiled paper
Propane tanks or cylinders
Aerosol cans that aren't empty

Many communities have collection programs for household hazardous waste to reduce the potential harm posed by these chemicals.

**What are the most common items that I can
put into my curbside recycling bin?**

Cardboard
Paper
Food boxes
Mail
Beverage cans
Food cans
Glass bottles
Jars (glass and plastic)
Jugs
Plastic bottles and caps

Generally, these are the most commonly recycled items. Please confirm with your local recycling provider first before putting these items in your curbside recycling bin, however, since what is accepted depends on your area.

Are paper or plastic shopping bags better for the environment? How about reusable bags versus disposal bags?
We do not have information on the environmental benefits of paper versus plastic bags. We encourages consumers to:

Reduce the number of bags they use,
Reduce the number of bags they throw away after one use,
Reuse bags, and
Recycle bags when they can no longer be used.
Consumers also can reduce waste by using reusable shopping bags.

Glass

This symbol asks that you recycle the glass container. Please dispose of glass bottles and jars in a bottle bank, remembering to separate colours, or use your glass household recycling collection if you have one.

WHY CAN'T I RECYCLE SOME GLASS ITEMS?
Some types of glass do not melt at the same temperature as bottles and jars. If they enter the glass recycling process it can result in new containers being rejected. These items should be recycled separately - check with your local household waste recycling centre.

HOW TO RECYCLE GLASS BOTTLES AND JARS
Put lids and caps back on. This reduces the chance of them getting lost during the sorting process as they can be recycled separately.
Empty and rinse - a quick rinse will do. Leftover liquid can contaminate other recyclables which may mean they aren't recycled.

Aluminium

This symbol indicates that the item is made from recyclable aluminium.

HOW TO RECYCLE

Rinse or wipe off any crumbs or food residue from foil trays. To rinse just dunk the tray in the washing up water - no need to run the tap.

Scrunch kitchen foil, tub and pot lids and wrappers together to form a ball - the bigger the ball, the easier it is to recycle.

As well as foil, you can usually recycle these other aluminium items:

Drinks cans
Screw top lids from bottles
(recycle with the bottle - the cap can be left on)
Takeaway containers and barbeque trays.

Symbol#1: PET or PETE

PET or PETE (polyethylene terephthalate) is the most common plastic for sin-gle-use bottled beverages, because it›s inexpensive, lightweight, and easy to recycle. It poses low risk of leaching breakdown products. Its recycling rates remain relatively low (around 20%), even though the material is in high demand by manufacturers.

Found in:
Soft drinks, water, ketchup mouthwash bottles; peanut butter containers; salad dressing and vegetable oil containers

How to recycle it:
PET or PETE can be picked up through most curbside recycling programs as long as it›s been emptied and rinsed of any food. When it comes to caps, our environmental pros say it's probably better to dispose of them in the trash (since they›re usually made of a different type of plastic), unless your town explicitly says you can throw them in the recycle bin. There›s no need to remove bottle labels because the recycling process separates them.

Recycled into:
Polar fleece, fiber, tote bags, furniture, carpet, paneling, straps, bottles and food containers (as long as the plastic being recycled meets purity standards and doesn›t have hazardous contaminants)

Symbol#2: HDPE

HDPE (high density polyethylene) is a versatile plastic with many uses, especially when it comes to packaging. It carries low risk of leaching and is readily recyclable into many types of goods.

Found in: Milk jugs; juice bottles; bleach, detergent, and other household cleaner bottles; shampoo bottles; some trash and shopping bags; motor oil bottles; butter and yogurt tubs; cereal box liners

How to recycle it: HDPE can often be picked up through most curbside recycling programs, although some allow only containers with necks. Flimsy plastics (like grocery bags and plastic wrap) usually can't be recycled, but some stores will collect and recycle them.

Recycled into: Laundry detergent bottles, oil bottles, pens, recycling containers, floor tile, drainage pipe, lumber, benches, doghouses, picnic tables, fencing, shampoo bottles

Symbol#3: PVC or V

PVC (polyvinyl chloride) and V (vinyl) is tough and weathers well, so it's commonly used for things like piping and siding. PVC is also cheap, so it's found in plenty of products and packaging. Because chlorine is part of PVC, it can result in the release of highly dangerous dioxins during manufacturing. Remember to never burn PVC, because it releases toxins.

Found in: Shampoo and cooking oil bottles, blister packaging, wire jacketing, siding, windows, piping

How to recycle it: PVC and V can rarely be recycled, but it's accepted by some plastic lumber makers. If you need to dispose of either material, ask your local waste management to see if you should put it in the trash or drop it off at a collection center.

Recycled into: Decks, paneling, mud-flaps, roadway gutters, flooring, cables, speed bumps, mats

Symbol#4: LDPE

LDPE (low density polyethylene) is a flexible plastic with many applications. Historically, it hasn't been accepted through most American recycling programs, but more and more communities are starting to accept it.

Found in: Squeezable bottles; bread, frozen food, dry cleaning, and shopping bags; tote bags; furniture

How to recycle it: LDPE is not often recycled through curbside programs, but some communities might accept it. That means anything made with LDPE (like toothpaste tubes) can be thrown in the trash. Just like we mentioned under HDPE, plastic shopping bags can often be returned to stores for recycling.

Recycled into: Trash can liners and cans, compost bins, shipping envelopes, paneling, lumber, landscaping ties, floor tile

Symbol#5: PP

PP (polypropylene) has a high melting point, so it's often chosen for containers that will hold hot liquid. It's gradually becoming more accepted by recyclers.

Found in: Some yogurt containers, syrup and medicine bottles, caps, straws

How to recycle it: PP can be recycled through some curbside programs, just don't forget to make sure there's no food left inside. It's best to throw loose caps into the garbage since they easily slip through screens during recycling and end up as trash anyways.

Recycled into: Signal lights, battery cables, brooms, brushes, auto battery cases, ice scrapers, landscape borders, bicycle racks, rakes, bins, pallets, trays

Symbol#6: PS

PS (polystyrene) can be made into rigid or foam products — in the latter case it is popularly known as the trademark Styrofoam. Styrene monomer (a type of molecule) can leach into foods and is a possible human carcinogen, while styrene oxide is classified as a probable carcinogen. The material was long on environmentalists' hit lists for dispersing widely across the landscape, and for being notoriously difficult to recycle. Most places still don't accept it in foam forms because it's 98% air.

Found in: Disposable plates and cups, meat trays, egg cartons, carry-out containers, aspirin bottles, compact disc cases

How to recycle it: Not many curbside recycling programs accept PS in the form of rigid plastics (and many manufacturers have switched to using PET instead). Since foam products tend to break apart into smaller pieces, you should place them in a bag, squeeze out the air, and tie it up before putting it in the trash to prevent pellets from dispersing.

Recycled into: Insulation, light switch plates, egg cartons, vents, rulers, foam packing, carry-out containers

Symbol#7: MISCELLANEOUS

A wide variety of plastic resins that don't fit into the previous categories are lumped into this one. Polycarbonate is number seven plastic, and it's the hard plastic that has worried parents after studies have shown it as a hormone disruptor. PLA (polylactic acid), which is made from plants and is carbon neutral, also falls into this category.

Found in: Three- and five-gallon water bottles, bullet-proof materials, sunglasses, DVDs, iPod and computer cases, signs and displays, certain food containers, nylon

How to recycle it: These other plastics are traditionally not recycled, so don't expect your local provider to accept them. The best option is to consult your municipality's website for specific instructions.

Recycled into: Plastic lumber and custom-made products

Compostable

Compostable

Products certified to be industrially compostable according to the European standard EN 13432/14955 may bear the 'seedling' logo.

Never place compostable plastic into the recycling with other plastics; as it is designed to break down it cannot be recycled and contaminates recyclable plastics. Plastics that carry this symbol can be recycled with your garden waste through your local authority.

RECYCLE & REUSE
electrical goods

Waste electricals

This symbol explains that you should not place the electrical item in the general waste. Electrical items can be recycled through a number of channels.

CANADA GOLD BEAVER BADGE

Participate in our Online Classes to earn these exclusive digital badges!
www.toptenaward.org

Design & Development by:
Tara Asadi

CANADA BRONZE BEAVER BADGE

Participate in our Online Classes to earn these exclusive digital badges!
www.toptenaward.org

Design & Development by:

Tara Asadi

1- How do you determine if a plastic container is recyclable?
A) Look at the number on the bottom
B) Look at the shape - only bottles, jugs and round dairy tubs are recyclable
C) Look at the color of the plastic
ANSWER:

2- How many pounds of food and food-soiled paper does the average King County household throw away each week?
A) 5
B) 9
C) 15
ANSWER:

3- How much of the contents of our dustbins could be easily recycled or composted?
A) 20%
B) 50%
C) 80%
D) 72%
E) 61%
ANSWER:

4- If you bring a lunch from home, how can you pack a "Waste Free lunch"? Tell us one way that you would prepare a waste free lunch box.
A) Pack food in durable, reusable containers.
B) Bring a drink in a durable, reusable container.
C) Pack the lunch in a durable, reusable box or bag.
D) All of the above
ANSWER:

5- It is predicted that we will run out of landfill space by___?
A) 2024
B) 2022
C) 2028
D) 2030
ANSWER:

6-Landfill sites are sites where waste is disposed of by burying it in the ground. In 2016 ____% of all the UK's waste went to landfill?
A) 37%
B) 50%
C) 66%
D) 24%
ANSWER:

7- Name one product that paper is recycled into after it goes in a recycling bin. Any of the following answers is correct:
A) Cardboard
B) more paper
C) paper towels
D) All of the above
ANSWER:

8- On average, each person in the U.K will throw away how much rubbish in 7 weeks?
A) 10kg
B) 40kg
C) Their own weight
D) 5kg
ANSWER:

9- Tell us about one way that you can reduce paper use at school or at home.
A) Use the back sides of each piece of paper
B) Double-sided photocopying or printing
C) Use each page in our notebooks

D) All of the above
ANSWER:

10- What are the 3 R's of waste management?
A) Reduce, Reuse, Recycle.
B) Refuse, Reduce, Recycle.
C) Rehome Recycle, Repair
D) All of the above
ANSWER:

11- What are the two largest components of a typical school's garbage?
A) Bottle caps
B) Paper
C) Food Scraps
D) b & C is correct
ANSWER:

12- What happens to food that is put into yard waste carts or into a school composting container?
A) The food scraps go to a special food-only landfill
B) The food scraps are made into new food
C) It's turned into compost that can be used to nourish our gardens
ANSWER:

13- What of the following can you put in your yard waste/food scrap bin?
A) Banana peel
B) Meat scraps and bones
C) Moldy cheese
D) Potato peelings
E) All of the above
ANSWER:

14- When recycling a plastic water bottle, what should you do with the cap?

A) The cap goes into a garbage can and the bottle goes in a recycling bin
B) Screw the cap back on the bottle, then put the bottle and cap in a recycling bin
C) Recycle the cap separately.
ANSWER:

15- Where does your garbage go when the waste hauler collects it?
A) It goes to the ocean, where it's dumped into the ocean.
B) It goes to a garbage transfer station, then to the Cedar Hills Regional Landfill
C) It goes to San Juan Island to be buried.
ANSWER:

16- Which of the following can NOT be placed in a school composting container or in your yard waste cart at home?
A) Apple core
B) Milk carton
C) Pizza delivery box
D) Paper napkins
ANSWER:

17- Which of the following food-soiled papers should you not put in the food scrap composting or yard waste bin?
A) Paper towels
B) Paper napkins
C) Greasy cardboard pizza delivery boxes
D) Plastic cups, utensils and plates
ANSWER:

18- Which of the following items belong in the garbage container?
A) A Ziploc baggy
B) A bottle cap
C) A straw
D) All of the above
ANSWER:

19- Which ONE of the following items DOES belong in the blue recycling container?
A) Food scraps such as a banana peel
B) A plastic bottle
C) A straw
D) A bottle cap
ANSWER:

20- Can you place broken window glass and unwanted ceramic dishes in the recycling bin?
A) Yes
B) No
ANSWER:

21- Can you place magazines and glossy advertising or junk mail in the recycling bin?
A) Yes
B) No
ANSWER:

22- Can you recycle a steel can, a glass bottle or a plastic bottle with the label on?
A) Yes
B) No
ANSWER:

23- Can you recycle Styrofoam trays and plastic utensils?
A) Yes
B) No
ANSWER:

24- Do staples have to be removed before recycling paper?
A) Yes
B) No
ANSWER:

CANADA SILVER BEAVER BADGE

Participate in our Online Classes to earn these exclusive digital badges!
www.toptenaward.org

Design & Development by:

Tara Asadi

Bibliography:

Abramovitz, J.1998. Taking a stand: Cultivating a new relationship with the world's forests. Washington DC., Worldwatch 140: 84 p.

Agency (742-R-94-001 April).

Ahmad, M. 1998. Eco-Labeling of Indonesian Timber and Timber Products. Manila, Asian Development Bank, 13p.

Amount of Fraud. Journal of Law and Economics 16, 67-88.

Andrews, R.N.L. 1998. Environmental regulation and business 'self-regulation'. Policy Sciences 31(3): 177-197.

Apodaca, Julia, "Market Potential of Organically Grown Cotton as a Niche Crop." Natural Fibers Research and Information Center, Bureau of Business Research, University of Texas at Austin, Paper presented at the Beltwide Cotton Conference in Nashville, TN, January 1992.

Asadi, J., "International Environmental Labelling, Economic Consequencies, Export Magazine, July 2001

Asadi, J. 2008. Mobile Phone as management systems tools, ISO Magazine, Vol.8, No.1

Asadi, J., Eco-Labelling Standards, National Standard Magazine, Sep. 2004.

Assocs., Cambridge MA and G. Davis, U. Tenn, Knoxville,TN. (68-W6-0021): xiii+76+226pp.

Balter, M. 1999. Scientific cross-claims fly in continuing beef war. Science (May 28) 284: 1453-1455.

Belsley, D.A., Kuh, E., and Welsch, R.E. (1980), Regression Diagnostics, New York: John Wiley & Sons, Inc.

Birett, M. J. 1997. Encouraging Green Procurement Practices in Business: A Canadian Case Study in Program Development (108-118). in Greener Purchasing : Opportunities and Innovation. Sheffield, Greenleaf Publishing 325p.

Bowen, Nicola, World Agrochemical Markets, PJB Publications Ltd., March 1991.

Burnside, A., (1990), Keen on Green, Marketing, 17 May, pp35-36

Butler, D., (1990), A Deeper Shade of Green, Management Today, June, pp74-79

Cairncross, F. 1995. Green, Inc.: A guide to business and the environment. London, Earthscan. 277p.

Cason, T. N. and L. Gangadharan, (2002), Environmental Labeling and Charter, M. (ed.) 1992. Greener marketing: a responsible approach to business. Sheffield, Greenleaf Publishing 403p.

Chemical Week, 1999. Europe's Beef Ban Tests Precautionary Principle. (August 11).

CHOI, J.P. Brand Extension as Informational Leverage. Review of Eco- nomic Studies, Vol. 65 (1998), pp. 655-669.

Conway, G. 2000. Genetically modified crops: risks and promise.

Corrado, M., (1989), The Greening Consumer in Britain, MORI, London

Corrado, M., (1997), Green Behaviour – Sustainable Trends, Sustainable Lives?, MORI, london, accessed via countries. Manila, Asian Development Bank 33p.

Cropper, M.L., L.D. Deck, and K.E. McConnell. "On the choice of Functional Forms for Hedonic Price Functions," Review of Economics and Statistics 70(1988): 668-675.

Darbi, M. R. and E. Karni, (1973), Free Competition and the Optimal

Davis, G. 1998. Environmental Labeling Issues, Policies, and Practices Worldwide. Washington, DC. EPA, 216p.

Dawkins, K. 1996. Eco-labeling: consumer's right-to-know or restrictive business practice? Minneapolis, Minn., Institute for Agriculture and Trade Policy.

Di Leva, C. E. 1998. International Environmental Law and Development. Georgetown Interna. Environ. Law Review 10 (2): 502-549.

Economics and Management 43, 339-359.

Eiderstroem, E. 1997. Eco-labeling: Swedish Style. Forum for Applied Research in Public Policy 141(4).

Elkington, J. and Hailes, J. 1990. The green consumer guide: You can buy products that don't cost the earth. New York, Viking Press. 96p.

EMONS, W. Credence Goods and Fraudulent Experts. RAND Journal of Economics, Vol. 28 (1997), pp. 107-119.

EMONS, W. Credence Goods Monopolists. International Journal of In- dustrial Organization, Vol. 19 (2001), pp. 375-389.

Environment Canada 1997. Towards Greener Government Procurement: An Environment Canada Case Study (pp. 31-46). in Greener Purchasing: Opportunities and Innovations.

Environmental Protection Agency 742-R-98-009, (1998),

Environmentalist 17 (2): 125-133.

Erskine, C.C. and Collins, L. 1996. Eco-labeling in the EU: a comparative study of the pulp and paper industry in the UK and Sweden. European Environment 17 (2) : 40-47.

Erskine, C.C. and Collins, L. 1997. "Eco-labeling: Success or failure?".

Ethical Consumer, (1995), Co-op Supermarkets take up Ethics, EC36, June/July, p4

Ethical Consumer, (June 1996), Green Cons, EC41, June, p5

European Communities, Commission of the, 1996. Eco-label revision.

European Communities, Commission of the. 1996. Conservation of West Africa's forests through certification. UN Courier 157: 71-73.

FAO, 1999. State of the World's Forests 1999.

FAO, 1999. Wood Fuel Surveys.

Feenstra, R.C. "Exact Hedonic Price Indexes," Review of Economics and Statistics 77 (1995): 634-653.

Feenstra, R.C., and J.A. Levinsohn. "Estimating Markups and Market Conduct with Multidimensional Product Attributes," Review of Economic Studies (62 (1995): 19-52.

Forest Stewardship Council: "Principles and criteria for forest stewardship" Document 1.2: <http://www.fscoax.org>

Forsyth, K. 1999. Will consumers pay more for certified wood products? Journal of Forestry 97 (2) : 18-22.

Freeman, A. M III. The Measurement of Environmental and Resource Values. Theory and Methods. Washington D.C.: Resource for the Future, 1993.

Friends of the Earth, 1993. Timber certification and eco-labeling. London, FOE:

Graves, P., J.C. Murdoch, M.A. Thayer, and D. Waldman. "The Robustness of Hedonic Price Estimation: Urban Air Quality," Land Economics 64(1988): 220-233.

Halvorsen, R. and R. Palmquist. "The Interpretation of Dummy Variables in Semilogarithmic Equations." American Economic Review 70:474-75 (1980).

Imhoff, Dan, and Grose, Lynda, and Carra, Roberto., "Organic Cotton Exhibit," Mimeo. Simple Life and distributed the Texas Organic Cotton Marketing Cooperative, O'Donnell, Texas (1996).

Imhoff, Dan. "Growing Pains: Organic Cotton Tests the Fiber of Growers and Manufacturers Alike," reprinted on Simple Life's web page (simplelife.com), but first printed by Farmer to Farmer, December 1995.

Incomplete Consumer Information in Laboratory Markets. Journal of Environmental labeling.

ISO 14020, ISO 14021,ISO 14024,ISO 14025, International Organization for Standardization.

Kennedy, P.E. "Estimation with Correctly Interpreted Dummy Variables in Semilogarithmic Equations," American Economic Review 71: 801 (1981).

Kirchho®, S., (2000), Green Business and Blue Angels.

Kraus, Jeff. Lab Technician at the North Carolina School of Textiles.

Labeling Issues, Policies and Practices Worldwide.

Lamport, L. 1998. The cast of (timber) certifiers: who are they? International J. Ecoforestry 11(4): 118-122.

Large Scale impoverishment of Amazonian forests by logging and fire. 1999.

Lathrop, K.W. and Centner, T.J. 1998. Eco-labeling and ISO 14000: An analysis of US regulatory systems and issues concerning adoption of type II standards. Environmental

Lee, J. et al. 1996. Trade related environmental measures; sizing and comparing impacts.

Lehtonen, Markku. 1997. Criteria in Environmental Labeling: A comparative Analysis on Environmental Criteria in Selected Labeling Schemes. Geneva, UNEP. 148p.

LIEBI, T. Trusting Labels: A Matter of Numbers? Working Paper Uni versity of Bern, No. 0201 (2002).

Lindstrom, T. 1999. Forest Certification: The View from Europe's NIPFs. Journal of Forestry 97(3): 25-31. London

Losey, J.E., Rayor, L.S. & Carter, M.E. 1999. Transgenic pollen harms monarch larvae. Nature 399 20 May): p.214.

Management 22 (2) : 163-172.

Mattoo, A. and H. V. Singh, (1994), Eco-Labelling: Policy Considera-

Michaels, R. G., and V. K. Smith. "Market Segmentation And Valuing Amenities With Hedonic Models: The Case Of Hazardous Waste Sites," Journal of Urban Economics, 1990 28(2), 223-242.

Mintel, (1991), The Green Consumer I, May

Mintel, (1994), The Green Consumer, Mintel Special Report

Moraga-Gonzalez, J. L. and N. Padr¶on-Fumero, (2002),

NCC, (1996a), Green Claims – a consumer investigation into marketing claims about the environment,

NCC, (1996b), Shades of Green – consumers' attitudes to green shopping, National Consumer Council,

Nelson , P."Information and Consumer Behaviour," Journal of Political Economy 78 (1970): 311-329..

Nicholson-Lord, D., (1993) 'Tis the Season to be Green, The Independent, 20 December

Nuttall, N., (1993), Shoppers can cross green products off their lists, The Times, 3 July

OCDE/GD(97)105. Paris, OECD. 81p.

OECD. "Ec-labelling: Actual Effects of Selected Programmes," OCDE/GD (97) 105, 1997, Paris. (available on line at http://www.oecd.org/env/eco/books.htm#trademono)

OECD. 1997a. Case study on eco-labeling schemes. Paris, OECD (30 Dec):

OECD. 1997b. Eco-labeling: Actual Effects of Selected Programs.

Osborne, L. "Market Structure, Hedonic Models, and the Valuation of Environmental Amenities." Unpublished Ph.D. dissertation. North Carolina State University, 1995.

Osborne, L., and V. K. Smith. "Environmental Amenities, Product Differentiation, and market Power," Mimeo, 1997.

Ozanne, L.K. and Vlosky, R.P. 1996. Wood products environmental certification: the United States perspective". Forestry Chronicle 72 (2) : 157-165.

Palmquist, R. B., F. M. Roka, and T.Vukina. "Hog Operations, Environmental Effects, and Residential Property Values," Land Economics 73(1), (1997): 114-24.

Palmquist, R.B. "Hedonic Methods," in J.B Braden and C.D. Kolstad, eds. Measuring the Demand for Environmental Improvement. Amsterdam, NL: Elsevier, 1991.

Pento, T. 1997. Implementation of Public Green Procurement Programs (22-31) in Greener Purchasing: Opportunities and Innovations. Sheffield, Greenleaf Publ. 325 p.

Perloff, J. "Industrial Organization Lecture Notes," Mimeo. University of California at Berkeley (1985).

Plant, C. and Plant, J. 1991. Green business: hope or hoax? Philadelphia, New Society Publishers 136 p.

Polak, J. and Bergholm, K. 1997. Eco-labeling and trade: a cooperative approach (Jan.): Policy in a Green Market. Environmental and Resource Economics 22, 419-

Poore, M.E.D. et al. 1989. No timber without trees. London, Earthscan. 352p.

Raff, D. M.G., and M. Trajtenberg. "Quality-Adjusted Prices for the American Automobile Industry: 1906-1940." NBER Working Paper Series, Working Paper No. 5035, February 1995.

Rastogi, J. 1998. What's Behind the Label? Complexities of Certified Wood. Ecoforestry 13 (2): 38-42.

Roberts, J. T. 1998. Emerging global environment standards: prospects and perils. Journal of Developing Societies 14 (1): 144-163.

Rosen, S., "Hedonic Prices and Implicit Markets: Product Differentiation in Pure Competition." Journal of Political Economy. 82: 34-55 (1974).

Ross, B. 1997. Eco-friendly procurement training course for UN HCR. : 126 p.

Ryan, S., and Skipworth, M., (1993), Consumers turn their backs on green revolution, The Times, 4 April

Salzman, J. 1997. Informing the Green Consumer: The Debate over the Use and Abuse of Environmental Labels. Journal of Industrial Ecology 1 (2): 11-22.

Sanders, W. 1997. Environmentally Preferable Purchasing: The US Experience (946-960) in Greener Purchasing: Opportunities and Innovations. Sheffield, Greenleaf Publ. 325p.

Sayre, D. 1996. Inside ISO 14000: The competitive advantage of environmental management. Delray Beach FL., St. Lucie Press. 232p.

SHAPIRO, C. Premiums for High Quality Products as Returns to Reputa- tion. Quarterly Journal of Economics, Vol. 98, No. 4 (1983), pp. 659-680.

Stillwell, M. and van Dyke, B. 1999. An activists handbook on genetically modified organisms and the WTO. Washington DC., The Consumer's Choice Council: 20 p.

Teisl, M. F., B. Roe, and R. L. Hicks. "Can Eco-labels tune a market? Evidence from dolphin-safe labeling," Presented paper at the 1997 American Agricultural Economics Association Meetings, Toronto.

THE GERSEN, C. Psychological Determinants of Paying Attention to Eco- Labels in Purchase Decisions: Model Development and Multinational Vali- dation. Journal of Consumer Policy, Vol. 23, No. 4 (2000), pp. 285-313.

Tibor, T. and Feldman, I. 1995. ISO 14000: a guide to the new environmental management standards. Burr Ridge Ill., Irwin Professional Publ. 250 p.

Torre, I. de la, & Batker, D. K. (n.d.) 1999-2000. Prawn to trade: prawn to consume. Graham WA., Industrial Shrimp Action Network (isatorre@seanet.com), [and] Asia –Pacific Townsend, M. 1998. Making things greener: motivations and influences in the greening of manufacturing. Aldershot, England, Ashgate Publisher. 203p.

U.S. Environmental Protection Agency. National Water Quality Fact Inventory: 1990 Report to Congress. EPA 503-9-92-006, Apr. 1992.

UK Eco-labelling Board website, accessed via http://www.ecosite.co.uk/Ecolabel-UK/

US Environmental Protection Agency (EPA742-R-99-001): 40 p. <www.epa.gov/opptintr/epp>

US EPA, 1993. Determinants of effectiveness for environmental certification and labeling programs. Washington, D.C., US Environmental Protect

US EPA, 1993. Status report on the use of environmental labels worldwide. Washington, D.C., US Environmental Protection Agency (742-R-93-001 September).

US EPA, 1993. The use of life-cycle assessment in environmental labeling. Washington, D.C., US Environmental Protection Agency (742-R-93-003 September).

US EPA, 1998. Environmental labeling: issues, policies, and practices worldwide. Washington DC., Environmental Protection Agency, Pollution Prevention Division Prepared by Abt

US EPA, 1999. Comprehensive procurement guidelines (CPG) program. Washington, D.C., US Environmental Protection Agency: <www.epa.gov/cpg>

US EPA, 1999. Environmentally preferable purchasing program: Private sector pioneers: How companies are incorporating environmentally preferable purchases. Washington, D.C.,

USG, 1993. Federal acquisition, recycling, and waste prevention. Washington DC., Executive Order: (20 October).

USG, 1998. Greening the government through waste prevention, recycling, and federal acquisition. Washington, D.C., Executive Order 13101 (September).

Van der Grijp, N. 1998. The Greening of Public Procurement in the Netherlands (60-71) in Greener Purchasing: Opportunities and Innovations. Sheffield, Greenleaf Pub. 325 p.

Vanclay, J.K. 1996. Lessons from the Queensland rainforests: steps towards sustainability. J. Sustainable Forestry 3 (2/3): 1-25.

Vidal, J., (1993), Shopping for a paler shade of green, The Guardian, 7 April

Voluntary Overcompliance. Journal of Economic Behavior and Organization

Von Felbert, D. 1995. Trade, environment and aid. Paris, OECD Observer 195: 6-10.

Ward, H. 1997. Review of European Community and International Environmental Law 6 (2): 139-147.

Wasik, John, F. Green Marketing and Management: a Global Perspective, Blackwell Business: Cambridge, Mass, 1996.

West, K. 1995. Ecolabels: the industrialization of environmental standards. The Ecologist (Jan/Feb) 25: 16-20.

Worcester, R., (1995), Business and the Environment – in the aftermath of Brent Spar and BSE, MORI,

World Commission on Forests and Sustainable Development: Final Report. <http://iisd.ca/wcfsd>.

Zarrilli, S., V. Jha, and R. Vossenaar, eds. Eco-labelling and International Trade, St martin Press, Inc. New-York, 1997.

APPENDIX I

Recycling Codes

Recycling codes are used to identify the material from which an item is made, to facilitate easier recycling or other reprocessing. The presence on an item of a recycling code, a chasing arrows logo, or a resin code, is not an automatic indicator that a material is recyclable; it is an explanation of what the item is made of. Codes have been developed for batteries, biomatter/organic material, glass, metals, paper, and plastics.[citation needed] Various countries have adopted different codes. For example, the table below shows the polymer resin (plastic) codes. In the United States there are fewer, because ABS is placed with "others" in group 7.

A number of countries have a more granular system of recycling codes. For example, China's polymer identification system has seven different classifications of plastic, five different symbols for post-consumer paths, and 140 identification codes. The lack of a code system in some countries has encouraged those who fabricate their own plastic products, such as RepRap and other prosumer 3-D printer users, to adopt a voluntary recycling code based on the more comprehensive Chinese system.

RECYCLING CODES

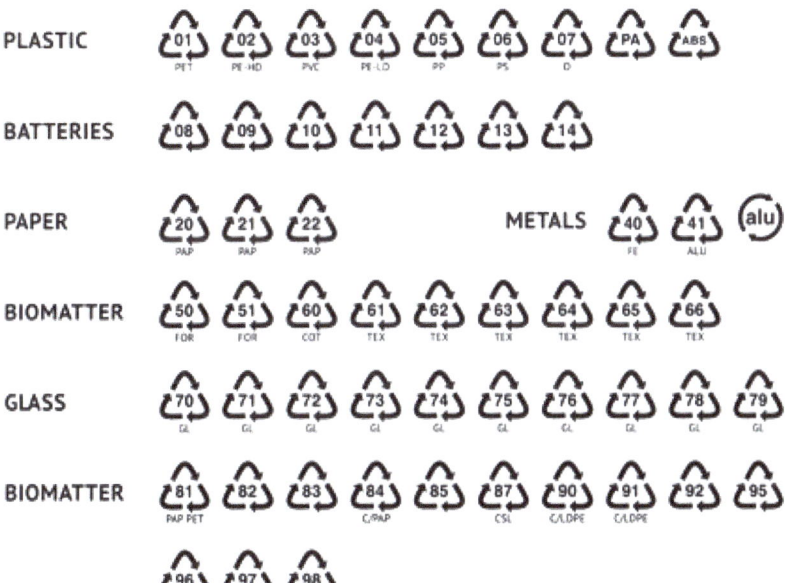

PLASTIC

| 01 PET | 02 PE-HD | 03 PVC | 04 PE-LD | 05 PP | 06 PS | 07 O | PA | ABS |

BATTERIES

| 08 | 09 | 10 | 11 | 12 | 13 | 14 |

PAPER

| 20 PAP | 21 PAP | 22 PAP |

METALS

| 40 FE | 41 ALU | (alu) |

BIOMATTER

| 50 FOR | 51 FOR | 60 COT | 61 TEX | 62 TEX | 63 TEX | 64 TEX | 65 TEX | 66 TEX |

GLASS

| 70 GL | 71 GL | 72 GL | 73 GL | 74 GL | 75 GL | 76 GL | 77 GL | 78 GL | 79 GL |

BIOMATTER

| 81 PAP PET | 82 | 83 | 84 C/PAP | 85 | 87 CSL | 90 C/LDPE | 91 C/LDPE | 92 | 95 |

| 96 | 97 | 98 |

ORGANIC   PAPER   PLASTIC   GLASS   METAL   E-WASTE   MIXED

PLEASE  RECYCLE

Environmental Lifestyle Guide

For Grade 9

For Grade 10

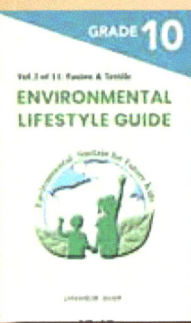
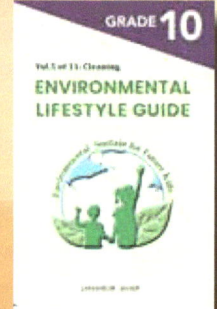
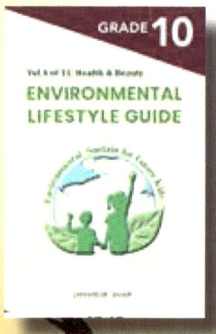

Plus Online Certification Tests via:
https://toptenaward.org

Standard Text Books

For Grade 11

For Grade 12

 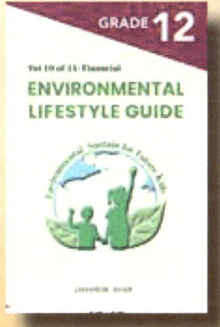 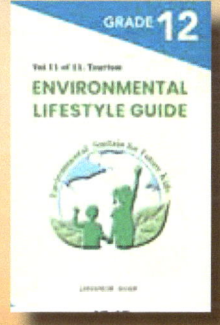

**Environmental Lifestyle Guide
Standard Text Book**
For Students Grade 9 to 12
Available in more than
39,000 Bookstores
all over the globe.
https://ecofriendlyeducation.com

Cooperation by:
Top Ten Award International Network
&
Environmental Sustain for Future Kids